GRIEF AND ECSTASY
RABHA ASHRY

This is a work of fiction. All names, characters, places, and incidents are a product of the author's imagination. Any resemblance to real events or persons, living or dead, is entirely coincidental.

Published by Akashic Books
©2023 Rabha Ashry
ISBN: 978-1-63614-124-4

All rights reserved
Printed in China
First printing

Akashic Books
Brooklyn, New York
Instagram, Twitter, Facebook: AkashicBooks
E-mail: info@akashicbooks.com
Website: www.akashicbooks.com

African Poetry Book Fund
Prairie Schooner
University of Nebraska
110 Andrews Hall
Lincoln, Nebraska 68588

TABLE OF CONTENTS

Preface by Malika Booker 5

disconnect 9
under the water 10
simmer 11
the same letter 12
crisis 13
a love letter to my worst enemy 14
breakfast 16
omission 17
salt and sunshine 19
to Michael 20
are you high? 21
still the girl 22
memorize 23
hungry, hungry 25
blue 27

Preface
by Malika Booker

Rabha Ashry's sparse lyric poems undulate and mesmerize. They explore liminal spaces and articulate the complicated physiological and psychological effects of existing "in-between doorways." There is a haunting, a silencing, a reckoning with love, faith, grief, and the limitation of language through observation and interrogation, yet there is no attempt at reconciliation. Instead, the poems dwell in the realm of limen, a sort of limbo poetics grappling with the reality of being an outsider, no doubt informed by Ashry's heritage, an Egyptian poet from Abu Dhabi based in Chicago.

> my heart heaves and I sing
> a snake charmer in a girl
>
> my fingers in knots, I can
> fall into the cartography
>
> of our ups and down
> of the in-between doorways
>
> ("the same letter")

Ashry grapples with the overwhelming task of writing during a global pandemic. Here the poet who is "too dry to fill a page" can only "stall and stutter." In the poem "disconnect," one of several *ars poetica* pieces in Ashry's collection, she deconstructs the art of writing or the struggle to find language "in my head / in this my emptiest year." There is such devastation in that last line, which eloquently captures the impact of the pandemic—its pathos and poignancy—while punching the reader in the gut.

In a number of poems, there is a silencing, where the poet is rendered "mute." For instance, in "crisis," "faith suddenly in question" leads the protagonist to "swallow my rebellion." While in the poem "omission" the protagonist confesses that "in every admission / I omit a true confession." Each encounter with this idea of self-muzzling builds an overarching motif of quietude as self-preservation, or culpability, and of utterance as resilience. Thus, silence and utterance are repeated themes that are manipulated to reaffirm the underlying importance of language (speech and written). This structural ambiguity is exploited in several poems where we encounter this echo:

> I sow my nails in grass
> dance to my sun
>
> loosen my moon tongue
>
> ("simmer")

Yet poems can simultaneously celebrate grief and ecstasy of speech. Take, for instance, "simmer," a poem that moves from an initial thematic brutal hush where we witness the I in the poem "simmer in water / my mouth full of sand / I offer myself up / for absolution / I stutter prayers . . ." to supplication, "may Allah let me into / the kingdom of heaven," to end with bliss. Structurally, the poem follows the rhythm and logic of prayer. In other poems like "still the girl" prayer becomes an anointment, an incantation, evoking delicate vulnerability and warmth through the action of palms and a whisper:

> I cradle your face
> late in the night
> whisper prayers for you

>   to myself
>   as you fall
>   asleep

("still the girl")

Ars poetica is another thematic hinge that constantly swings open. We meet it again with the poem "omission," which seems on one hand to be addressing the act of writing yet dissolves halfway through into a sonnet-like volta revealing a delicate ode to love, a lover, a loved one, or maybe an extended metaphor for writing. The confessional nature with its hesitant yet tender language, as well as the address to "you," invite layered textual interpretations and a sophisticated ambiguity. This device is willfully employed by Ashry.

> a lyric in
> the spaces   between lines
>
> my hair
> like an unfamiliar word
> in a language I used to speak
>
> and I come back to   tongues
> in every word there is a hunt
> there is a
>   "I could've told you already"

("omission")

Throughout the collection nature is used to convey heightened emotional states, and it is the spine through which the poet can navigate a massive emotional terrain: "bare branches reaching for the sky / my mouth a sunflower still blooming." The juxtapositioning of these images is what imbues a potent poignancy underlined with hope—the barren denoting bereft, a stripping away, a desolate state of being—contrasted immediately with the mouth of a sunflower still blooming. The reader will notice yet again the mention of mouth and its connotations with earlier observations.

My favorite poem is the elegiac verse simply titled "to Michael." Here Ashry uses tightly constrained lines to conduct a sanctified ceremony, a lyrical container for enacting a ritualized send off. She admirably enables the poem to present a litany of libations from "roll a cigarette in your name / light a candle & smoke a prayer," in order to bear witness to a final journey into water. Yet sentimentality or nostalgia is not encouraged in this moving memorial piece. Always in the midst of melancholy, this poet still manages to demonstrate that sadness often coexists with light.

Ashry cradles us in a poetic limbo, using sensuous and stark imagery to navigate the boundaries between grief and ecstasy.

disconnect

      small in my head wires
      disconnect words crash
      into each other
            and
            I am mute

      too dry to fill a page
      I   stall and stutter
      too hesitant to move
      too small

            in my head
      in this my emptiest year

under the water

watch the salt water aflame
only by moonlight
under the water

you are
quiet and unafraid

you are
silent and still

supplicant like a daughter

simmer

I simmer in water
my mouth full of sand

I offer myself up
for absolution

I stutter prayers
may Allah forgive me

may Allah let me into
the kingdom of heaven

I sow my nails in grass
dance to my sun

loosen my moon tongue

the same letter

I set fire to the same letter every night
I can hear the words behind your words

my heart heaves and I sing
a snake charmer in a girl

my fingers in knots, I can
fall into the cartography

of our ups and down
of the in-between doorways

like a mute, I offer you my hands
to read my palms

crisis

on a sweltering April afternoon
Abu Dhabi sidewalks radiating heat
I'm ensconced in the backseat of the Kia
with the busted AC and
the doors with the child lock

wrapped in two scarves out of piety
I catch my eye in the rearview mirror
my faith suddenly in question
I stop believing in God
for just a moment

my mom clumsily parks the car
outside the white block of concrete
with the green windows
she looks at me
and I'm flushed red with guilt

I swallow my rebellion
avert my gaze like a good daughter
I entreat Allah to forgive me
still holding my disbelief
close to my chest

a love letter to my worst enemy

I started dreaming about

running away a decade and a half
ago, and some goals you

do reach if you dream about them
long enough, so here I am

but where does that leave
you? I have spent lifetimes trying

for you. Where am I when it's not
with you? I'm here, on the couch

in my living room next to my dog.
behind on cleaning my room and

doing my laundry. Mine. Mine.
This is how I live without you.

This is how the days stack up
on top of each other since

I last saw you or heard
your voice. I can't tell you how

long it will be, this being away,
how long it will take. I can't tell you

that I don't miss you sometimes.
Sometimes I think about you but

there's nothing new to say, because
I want my world to remain foreign

and unreachable to you. You are not welcome
in it anymore and that is because I love you.

Maybe the same way you love me.

breakfast

my body grows softer and my hair grows longer
I look like the girl I've never been
my body a home I'm a stranger in
my girlhood a story I can't read

it's been a long winter
I feel my bare branches reaching for the sky
my mouth a sunflower still blooming

omission

this is a lie
only I gave up
for a win
I can't fathom

I sit here
pen in hand
like I'm
a lyric in
the spaces   between lines

my hair
like an unfamiliar word
in a language I used to speak

and I come back to   tongues
in every word there is a hunt
there is a
      "I could've told you already"

if I wrote a sonnet
about your yellow hair
you would know

in my dreams you understand

here's a messy recital
of everything I haven't learned to say

in everything I am afraid
in the colors
of every dress
I've worn for you

and in every admission
I omit a true confession

salt and sunshine

    you are my salt

        leave me with your morning eyes
    tell me "I'm just borrowing"
        when I'm just burrowing

    you planted me & I
    drowned in the mulch

    I want to be your wisteria
            your pocket knife

    will you douse me in vinegar?
    the seeds won't grow under my tongue

    you know about the crosshairs   the coils of my hair
        every word sacrificed to an unforgiving *god*

to Michael

the woman in the curtain watches me
in my bell pepper–red coat
I roll a cigarette in your name
light a candle & smoke a prayer

today I set three alarms for you
I watched three sisters hold each other
I packed a bowl while we raised a glass
witnessed your last journey into the sea

how fitting that you would come and go
with the waves, where else would we
find you? in my dreams by the beach
in love with every large body of water

I hope the salt water soothes your aches
I hope we share one more cigarette
(even if this time you only
gesture with it wildly in my mind)

are you high?

enough to look at the clouds

on a hot day in August
when we walk into the dark   glistening

me in my yellow dress
 drowning like the sun

I list every color in my room
not counting my sunset dress
              you watch me

we sleep to bedtime stories
              touching in the dark
dismembering and remembering

when the golden hour arrives
I watch myself in the mirror
and I know I have finally found
something heartbreaking

something beautiful
this quiet slow creation

still the girl

I cradle your face
late in the night
whisper prayers for you
to myself
      as you fall
           asleep

what terror strikes at night
that you   my love
could be fleeting
      could be another
"this too shall pass"

and I'm still the girl
writing these poems
a little high
      and a little terrified

I place a chrysanthemum over my mouth
and carve vines into my fingers

may every word
my tongue & the tips
of my fingers touch
be beautiful

may every touch
of my lips & my fingertips
against your freckled skin
be beautiful too

memorize

you on the phone right now
"I'll see you here in a little bit, love."
in your car practicing my chant

roll your r, let it travel
down your tongue
let it crown your lips

you love my words
you follow the lines
from one bed to another

your dexterous fingers
study my every letter
and you swallow them

so sweetly, opening to me
like a favorite book from summers ago
on a balcony somewhere else

you use sweet tobacco leaves
to roll our stanzas
touch them to my lips

let them get spicy
"baby," I tell you, "they're poison"
but you in the sun

with your hair alive around you
your closed eyes and delicious lips
you bring spring to my door

wake the green in my trees
watch my daisies bloom

hungry, hungry

spread out before you
like a feast
you are hungry   hungry   starving
ready to devour
  and   I
am falling into
your dilated Aegean
and you
       are
             drowning in
    my Nile

write an elegy for this exile
this girl/woman still
getting lost on her way home
gorge yourself on all
my dead ends

I purloin consonants
keep them under my tongue
this tongue you split in two
for me, for now just for me

sibilate just the last
syllable of my name
susurrate the beginning
sing it with me

still you are in your car

hands never on the
        steering wheel
reaching into me
your eyes an incoming tide

I'm looking down
and the world
spreads out before me
like a feast

blue

I find myself submerged in blue, the lake
warm and welcoming. Not just in the

morning, but at night too, your eyes
like falling. Your sweet face a slice of the moon,

your sunlight hair, the war
waging on streets near and far, the summer

of discontent. The summer we fall,
and it feels like flying. We both

wake up intermittently through the night
to whisper "I love you." Nights

when, restless, you leave our bed. Still,
I call your name and you're

by my side, soft. I open like a holy book
to you and you read all my pages.

Even when, between the two of us,
we misread the instructions and forget

your wallet again. Even when,
the call drops, hours into another long drive,

and, frustrated, I tell you, "this
is not okay." Still, you hold my hand,

kiss my psalms, love all the verses
I haven't written yet. Still, at the

end of the night, we rub our feet
together, soft and in love.